Swan Bones

Swan Bones

Bethany Bowman

RESOURCE *Publications* · Eugene, Oregon

SWAN BONES

Copyright © 2018 Bethany Bowman. All rights reserved. Except for brief quotations in critical publications or reviews, no part of this book may be reproduced in any manner without prior written permission from the publisher. Write: Permissions, Wipf and Stock Publishers, 199 W. 8th Ave., Suite 3, Eugene, OR 97401.

Resource Publications
An Imprint of Wipf and Stock Publishers
199 W. 8th Ave., Suite 3
Eugene, OR 97401

www.wipfandstock.com

PAPERBACK ISBN: 978-1-5326-5287-5
HARDCOVER ISBN: 978-1-5326-5288-2
EBOOK ISBN: 978-1-5326-5289-9

Cover Art: Kelly Louise Judd. Ten Swans. Pen and watercolor on paper, 2010.

The scripture quotations used in "Ram Offering" are from The ESV® Bible (The Holy Bible, English Standard Version®), copyright © 2001 by Crossway, a publishing ministry of Good News Publishers. Used by permission. All rights reserved." All other scripture verses are taken from the KJV.

Manufactured in the U.S.A.

For Mary Beth Gallogly

Contents

    Acknowledgments   ix

The River

    Signs   4
    Flying Cross   6
    Cardinal Moon   8
    Chickens   9
    Early Summer Prayer   11
    Lock 18   12
    Kukicha   13
    Alleys   15
    Indiana Breakers   16
    Dog at the Bus Stop   17
    The Pinecrest Years   18
    Vulture God   19
    Thanksgiving   20
    Gladys with the Stand Up Bass   24
    Allegany Prayer   25
    Tea   27
    Water   29
    Hawks   31
    The Musicians   32
    Slava   33

The Hills

Bees   36
Dresses   38
Cathy   41
Trestle   42
Fluff   43
Envy   44
Sarabache   46
Swan Bones   47
Song for Red Efts   49
Hats Off   50
Black Caps   51
Casey Road   54
Dineen's (After Fishing)   55
Red '86 Honda Nighthawk   57
Woman with Outstretched Arms   58
Potpourri   59
Casting on Loon Lake   60
Country Affair   61
Blueberries   63
Advent Ride   66

The Valley

Butterfly 68
Candles, Sugar, Rum 70
Marble City Breakdown 71
Wrestler 72
Blue Lens 73
Baptism 74
The Bell 75
Wood Sorrel 76
Luthier 77
Angelica 78
All Souls 79
Betty 81
Aunt Mary Stirs Coffee with Her Thumb 82
Communion 84
Windows 86
Shirley Jones and the Storm Cock 87
Ram Offering 89
Jiffy Lube Pam 91
My Parents Jitterbug at Weddings 92
Mohawk Valley 93

Acknowledgments

I would like to express gratitude to the editors of the following publications in which poems in this book first appeared, sometimes in different form.

Apple Valley Review: "Bees," "Envy"

Art House America: "Candles, Sugar, Rum," "Dresses," "Kukicha," "The Musicians"

Ascent: "Signs"

the Aurorean: "Indiana Breakers"

Blueline: "Advent Ride," "Casey Road"

The Comstock Review: "Swan Bones"

The Cresset: "Trestle," "Potpourri"

Kentucky Review: "Water"

The Lascaux Review: "My Parents Jitterbug at Weddings"

Lime Hawk: "Blueberries," "Early Summer Prayer," "Hawks"

Midwestern Gothic: "Alleys," "Flying Cross"

Nimrod International: "Cardinal Moon," "Gladys with the Stand Up Bass"

The Other Journal: "Wrestler"

Relief Journal: "Baptism," "Blue Lens," "Butterfly," "Communion"

Rock and Sling: "Allegany Prayer," "Black Caps"

Sapientia: "Ram Offering," "Wood Sorrel"

The Timberline Review: "Dog at the Bus Stop," "Tea"

The Tishman Review: "Marble City Breakdown," "Mohawk Valley," "The Pinecrest Years"

Windhover: "Slava"

Also, a special thank you to the following individuals who have spent time with these poems over the past few years and given meaningful advice along the way: Daniel Bowman Jr., Emily Whittaker, Amy and Jack Peterson, Julie Moore, Tania Runyan, Jae Newman, Marci Johnson, Hannah Dillon, Kathy and Timothy Dick, Beth Lykling, and Rachel Lake.

Thank you to the following professors for believing in me: Harold Hurley, Judd Decker, and Thom Ward.

Thank you to Orin Domenico for introducing me to Robert Johnson and Barbara Kingsolver, letting me read Blanche Dubois, and giving me the English scholarship even though I wanted to be a nurse. Thank you to the Bookouts for the marching band memories.

Thank you to Kelly Louise Judd for allowing me to use her beautiful illustration for cover art, and to Kelli Allen for my epigraph, a line from her poem "Market Day in Someone Else's City."

Finally, thank you to my family: Gail and Paul Whittaker, for unfailing support; Gabe, for country drives and birdwatches; Emily, for being the best of sisters; and Grandma Edith Gallogly, for passing down your love of books and giving me my first volume of poetry. Thank you to Dan, for endless encouragement, edits, and late night snacks, and to Una and Casey for being you. Thank you to my extended family for the gift of music, and to the Mohawk Valley friends who are family too, and always in my heart.

"Some towns are the wing bones we crush in our hands."

—Kelli Allen

The River

Signs

They know they've arrived when they see trees.
Trees mean water, timber, game. They unload the wagon,
eat flapjacks. Pa plays fiddle, phoebes sing.
Much later, our family drives five-hundred miles
from upstate New York to northern Indiana.
Vineyards line the Great Lakes; we don't stop.
Before long, it's soybeans and corn and no hills.
Somewhere near Columbus, the kids sample conies
with Cincinnati chili, and I wonder if I wrinkled my nose
the same way when my husband took the job.

Una counts buzzards while our youngest finally naps.
We listen to C. S. Lewis on audio book: *The Problem of Pain*.
Una's eyes close, and we discuss the new house,
afraid the wallpaper might be ancient, that the roof,
with its four layers, might not hold off tornado season rain.
We wonder if we've made the right decision,
uprooting the kids from their grandparents, the Valley,
to follow a dream that rubs legs and wings together
like locusts in the Midwest, and if there will be a sign
we've made the right choice, and if we'll recognize it
if it hums and snaps at dusk. Pa could read the signs,
but still, some nights, trudged home with a rifle
full of shells, empty pockets, no meat.

We wonder if it's right to look for signs,
knowing there's just one, The Sign of Jonas,
and the only way to wake up on a new shore
is to spend three days in the belly of a whale.
But there are signs: A doorbell that chimes *Auld Lang Syne*,
garden rife with onions, stray cat asleep on the porch.
Inside, the walls are damask, ceilings high,
and the staircase may lead to a magic wardrobe.

Best of all, there's room for the piano,
which I will teach our children to play
just as my mother taught me, and I will read to them
the books of my childhood, and pray,
in the spirit of Ma, who, miles from anywhere,
washed muslin and calico as though it mattered.

Flying Cross

> The silhouette of a Cooper's Hawk in flight is sometimes described as a "flying cross."
>
> —*Hawk Mountain*, raptor conservation organization

At breakfast, a stentorian crack
against the picture window
and the kids and I are up:
jam-faced, suddenly caffeinated.

A Cooper's hawk hunches over its prey—
probable relative of the starlings
we shared a house with last fall.

The small bird hangs limp as Jesus
in the accipiter's mouth
as its breath is squeezed out
a few feet from my bell feeder.

This happened before.
When we first moved, at Payne's,
British bistro in Gas City, Indiana:

Hawk drives small bird into French doors
as I savor grilled brie with bacon
try to forget, for a moment,
my life in Middle America.

Not that it's so bad—
this life with starlings.

They find their way in
through four layers of roof,
foramen where filigree pulls away
from dormer, into the attic and down
through century-old pocket doors.

Despite my husband's best efforts
with foam spray, we can't seem to
keep nature from waking us up here,
getting into our personal space, dreams.

It stuns us, drives us into the looking glass.
Only then does it mount on wings,
like a flying cross, glide us to heavenly places.

Cardinal Moon

Why a blood moon? Our five-year-old son
as we unroll sleeping bags onto wet grass.
Is it time to talk about the book of Joel—
portents, prophesies, the book of Revelation?

What's a tetrad? Our ten-year-old daughter
as I explain how Cassiopeia resembles a tornado,
what frightens us most in this Midwestern town.

Is it time to discuss numbers—consecutive
lunar eclipses, sixth seals and surreal dreams?
Why not a cardinal moon? A crabapple moon?
Firebush moon, ladybug moon, red wagon moon?

I relate the Rayleigh scattering of sunlight
through the atmosphere, how the moon
only *appears* to be red as Taylor Swift's
"Blank Space" blares from the garage radio.

Where does God live if the cosmos goes on forever?
If the Great Bear is a dipper, Southern Cross an umbrella,
I will lift mine eyes. Chew the moon slowly.

Hear every crunch as I scatter it in fall,
that perfect *pomme*, as wind dissipates dew
like a doe and her fawns spreading star-like carpels
and seeds or a red-crested bird, flitting monthly
from crescent to beautiful predictable feminine full moon.

Chickens

For Jack and Amy

My friend's husband is gentle.
He takes sugar ants outdoors in spring,
spends spare time learning chords
to pop songs big the year he was born.

But last summer when their pullets began
to disappear, his anger became fuel
for something else—a source: like uranium
for sun power or fission for energy.

He drowned the possum denning
under their porch; chucked its
bloated body in the back field
where they'd once tried to keep bees.

A few days later, the carcass was covered
in vultures. My friend hoped they'd pick it
to bones, didn't want her kids to know
that like Cain, they'd taken an innocent life.

(The brood was gone without blood
or feathers. Only a hawk could have
accomplished such a thing.)

But the vultures left the dead alone;
apparently hog cholera's easier to digest
than swollen possum. Husband away at school,
my friend mowed circles around it for weeks.

Maybe next year they'll try an orchard, a garden.
Their apples won't be scabby, get crown gall
or fire blight, and the cherry tomatoes—
God they'll be small and red

and we'll pop them into our mouths
like atomic fire balls, seeds and juice
exploding, mushroom clouds rising
as we watch the sun go down in the country.

Early Summer Prayer

The gray bobbed woman
calls common loons
with her hands at the bonfire,
lips pressed to thumbs.
Fingers open, close,
up and down like a kestrel's tail
or blue fan in the relief
at the lower northern portico
of Hatshepsut's temple.
In a boat the queen fishes,
fowls in kilt and crown
for as long as the colors
hold true or until the usurper
erases her inscriptions.
Like the first female pharaoh,
the gray woman would like
to remove the feminine "t"
from the end of her name
or float into some tundra pond,
evicting territorial owners.
Instead she'll moan
as smoke and early summer
ascend like red granite obelisks,
each rich yodel a prayer
the pair will mate for life.

Lock 18

A flaming sword would block the perimeters
of our hometown and unlike the first couple,
we couldn't have been more corybantic.

Summers, constructing clay diyas we'd one day
fill with oil, light, and let loose on the Ganges
or any river wider than the Mohawk.

Winters, recreating silent films in the attic;
if our lives were black and white, at least
lips and violins, muted gestures, leitmotif.

You followed these dreams. Traveled, studied,
saw clearly the forces that shape the universe.
Or maybe nothing so Faustian, but you got out.

I broke covenant, stayed in the Valley:
waited tables, folded negligees. I learned
first names, favorite drinks, tastes in underthings.

The hills became sacrosanct with their cornflowers
and seasonal roads, during thunderstorms, coruscating.
At some point I stopped wishing for something else.

Kukicha

Twig tea. I sip you and I'm wild again,
bringing my master gifts.
I read that you're brewed in Liji,
just south of Kyoto,
from discarded stems, stalks,
leftovers from more rife greens;
that you're not a "true" tea.

This makes me sad.
How can anything so woody,
so vegetal emerge from waste,
have secrets to hide?
Clearly you come from the land
of *higuma*, the Hokkaido brown bear.

I'm in need of a near-death experience;
I will drink.
I'll put my trust in records,
since 1962: 86 attacks and 33 passings.

Steaming earth aromas.
I inhaled them while pregnant
and found myself singing
the song of a creek bed.
Brook trout so brown, like home,
one modest female mallard
swimming away from the bridge
with her mate, and yellow celandine—
blossoms I've known since childhood
which, if you rip the stem,
drip with nitid paint.

I will pick one when the rain falls.
This way, I'll have something to wash
from my skin before I begin to browse,
time to confess,
because once I'm born again
I will strip every bit of stiffness
from your branches,
caper with boastful wings,
disable a dreamer's voice box.

Only then, when my love's green head
lies calm and still, will I deliver him back,
tenderly, to the cement block steps
of the porch he will finish someday.

Alleys

Behind our back yard, an alley: Daily beat
of our neighborhood's resident derelict.
He pursues cans and bottles,
tells my husband to fuck off, sings.
Stray cats visit us here too.
They pounce on day lily reeds,
hunt cicadas in our tangle of sweet peas.

This is not the hardest thing we've dealt with
since the move from New York.
Mental illness has padded after us for years,
sometimes purring, always scratching,
most predictably, esurient as hell.

I've grown hungry too.
Tired of being exposed, trapped,
neutered, but not returned—
forbidden from keeping jungly garden,
junk cars, busted bikes out of sight.

I want to look my neighbors in the eye.
Sit up front in church. Join something;
the choir, ASPCA. Or better yet,
walk with my shadow man when night falls.
Reason with him. Legitimize him.
Hold his calloused hand as he screams at the world.

Indiana Breakers

For Suzie

It's a good day to paint. She has a clear view of the courthouse,
bulwark of this Midwestern town with its bell and postcard austerity.
Winter aconite, tiny yellow flowers which generally pop by Lent
have finally scaled snow. Honeybees are all over them.

Library goers, antique-shop prowlers, two police officers stop.
They are the heart of this place—heroes who care about art,
church, flowers. But they don't comprehend her canvas.

The abandoned storefront she captures was once a five-and-dime.
Vacant for decades, the floor has caved and despite its
pressed tin ceiling, cherry wainscoting, no one's going to save it.

Starlings flit in and out of clefts. Two lie dead in the rubble.
Birds dart into the belfry of the courthouse too, but it's the
sunken joists of the store which seem to swell when morning
light bends, approximating waves off the coast of Kittery.

She won't complete the work. By May, bricks and tile will fall,
town will vote and building will be condemned and razed.
The artist may or may not return to Maine, and the courthouse,
as always, will stand fettered with flags, heritage roses on the Fourth.

Dog at the Bus Stop

We meet on the steps of the old church
on the corner of Main and Mechanic.
The chill is bitter—temperature
hasn't climbed out of the single digits.
The moon, waning gibbous, shines crisply
at 7 a.m., desperate as the wash
our Amish neighbors hang,
little to no hope of sun.

I dread the morning trek,
though our destination is only
a few blocks from the first floor
of the drafty Victorian we call home.
I wake the baby, wrap him in blankets,
shoulder him; stroller can't cut through snow
and the Caterpillar seldom plows early.

I even dread the kids:
one always without gloves
in some threadbare sweatshirt.
I'm perpetually taking off my mittens
to zip it; his hands are too cold,
mother too busy with little ones to notice.

Suddenly a dog bounds across the park
past shrouded swings, open buggy
over three feet of snow, straight for us
and Luke's laughing; he hugs that dog
for all he's worth, slips down ice-covered steps
to run lubberly around parking lot in soused sneakers
with this wet, wonderful, beacon of a dog,
past bed and breakfast, another vacant church,
curdled Victorian which, twelve gas valve
leaks later, will burn to the ground before spring.

The Pinecrest Years

For Katharine

Shaking the sheets with Estella,
cold-sound patter of bare feet

returning from the cellar—
bedtime palace of little girls too old

to snatch pancakes from the stovetop,
too young to hate spiders in their nets.

But we killed them,
braided them into our hair,

wrote them into our heroes,
fed them to gray squirrels asleep in the snow.

Vulture God

Psalm 17:8

Bald-headed scavenger, augury of death:
You pee down your legs to cool off,
vomit when rattled to lighten your load.
Make no distinction between cow carcass,
laced with chemicals, and Parsi high priest.

But some mornings, on backroads
as sun cuts through Indiana fog
your shoulders unlax and you cross
from field to field—in flight, formidable.
The tips of your feathers are opera gloves.

Hide me in the shadow of your wings.

And those under-the-table scraps
I can't comprehend: the way you made
that woman work for it, said the law is still with us—
law that condemns, stones, divides
whole people groups from their sisters . . .

Even in horaltic pose, are you ever truly sanitized?

But some mornings you break that law,
heal with spit and stripes, make no distinction
between town slut and virgin mother.
Blessed be your hooked nose, receding hairline,
circles in the fog waiting for my heart to soften.

Thanksgiving

I drive for the service.
Not for turkey or even family,
but for eighty-year old sopranos
with swivel gun vibratos
who seem to believe,
as they belt "The Battle Hymn,"
that their feet aren't arthritic
and corn-ridden, but *swift, jubilant.*

I drive for Don Fenner,
spindly in tricot and breeches,
reading this year's proclamation
from our first black president
who seems to believe,
despite acute racial tensions
and cultural disseverance,
in a "reservoir of goodness,"
in "Amazing Grace."

Even George Washington,
after reconnoitering forts
and revolutionaries, stood
in this limestone church, called
the Mohawk Valley beautiful.

Mrs. N. is beautiful—
older, but dignified
with teased dyed hair,
bright red scarf, lips.
I wonder if her son still sings.

Indiana's grown on me.
I've sung my heart out
at a Warrant concert
under the *Miami Indian* sculpture
used in the opening credits
of *Parks and Rec*, reveled
in the irony of a church sign
across the parking lot,
proffering the wages of sin.

I've stared down a rat snake
at pyramids called mounds,
built by the Adena-Hopewell people,
tried to imagine what its ancestors
thought of the turn of the century
carnival rides—wooden coaster
called "Leap the Dips"—which
strangely preserved the earthworks.

Other things are harder
to reconcile: a racist slur
at my son's soccer game,
Confederate flags that
mean more than fierce
independence or a middle
finger raised to The Man.

I want my children to understand
tension. To hold it firmly,
but gently in open hands,
recognize it in their own souls.

We sit through a slide show
of Edgar Heap of Birds'
signage installations,
including *Building Minnesota*,
which honors the Dakota Sioux
hanged by Lincoln and Johnson
in our nation's largest mass execution.
Some accounts say the men held hands.

Most holidays, we drink craft beer,
listen to Sufjan Stevens'
zombie Christmas album,
try to ignore our neighbors,
who seem to have nothing better to do
than light fireworks under Chuck Taylors.

But this year we'll trudge through Toledo,
Cleveland, Buffalo for the service,
chance to catch a whiff of Mrs. N's cologne;
for blue collar folks who take pride
in a priest and rabbi sharing a pulpit.

According to the marker,
Washington once took a meal
where my brother and I
now walk off pie in wet snow

and I think: Does everyone know
to the second when their heart
became a vacant lot where
someone memorable
once spent the night?

After an hour or so, we'll return
to the house I grew up in.
My father will show me the
scrapbook he's working on;
one of his sisters has already
put in a request to tidy up history.[1]

---

1. President Obama quoted Marilynne Robinson's phrase, "Reservoir of Goodness" when delivering the eulogy for Charleston pastor and senator, the Reverend Clementa Pinckney, in June of 2015.

Gladys with the Stand Up Bass

Her ghost, 5-feet 2, fat, in pin curls
plucks *Red Wing* Saturday nights
at the grange, bass fiddle big as
her laugh, her "glad ass,"
family, North Country nights.

Play a tune for me, Gladys;
something fast, a jitterbug.
Play me the sledding hill
before the talc mine,
marble churches
when the mines pulled out.

Play me a slow one, Gladys;
an end-of-the-nighter.
Play me Grandpa before
black lung—licking sumac,
planting moonflowers,
pointing out stars:

This one a stand up bass,
this one a couple in foxtrot,
this one a woman
just 5-feet-2, fat,
in a country print dress
plucking *Red Wing*.

Allegany Prayer

I want to love you, women of the Southern Tier—
to embrace your vocalizations:
recognize slate, know aluminum.

But every call you sound is friction,
sliding lid across the surface of a box,
push and pull, cut and cackle, cry.

My son can't sleep. There are ghosts
in the house. *Pray for me.*

A gay man lived here. *Jesus.*

An EMS van. *Lord.*

I want to love you, women of the Southern Tier—
to embrace your colors:
recognize jade, know carnelian.

But every prayer's a leaf that's turning,
fading yellow, bleeding red,
fallen, fueled, lit and smoking.

They're all mixed up. *Jesus.*
They're not like us. *Lord.*

Snip and saw, bend and break, boast.

Hear that male? I'll make him strut.
With my mouth I'll call him out.
My daughter knows who made the sky,
reason why the savior died:

for all our sins.

I want to love you, women of the Southern Tier—
to grow old together like trees in autumn,
crimson of sumac, browns of oak;
made perfect by cooler nights, warm sunlight,
by waste still clinging from summer.

Tea

A few years back, neither of us would have left the Valley.
We'd have married our high school sweethearts.
We'd be poor. Our husbands would drink,
but my kids would husk corn on your back porch
in bare, unblemished feet. I'd teach yours piano:
All Cows Eat Grass, Every Good Boy Does Fine.

We'd meet once a month: auxiliary, temperance society,
quilting, canning, sewing circle, hymn sing.

There'd be Christmas caroling and midnight mass,
homespun gifts, voices raised around the fire.
There would be no need to escape for a few hours
on New Years, to a snowmobile bar that will charge
five bucks to hear some shitty Metallica cover band.

I wouldn't live in a state I know nothing about;
you wouldn't be hundreds of miles away.
Our daughters would be more than pen pals.
You'd not spend the night discussing anti-depressants,
how they've ruined your sex life—
how you can decipher the call of barn owl from barred,
but cannot, by God, figure out why your husband
spends all of his time on the internet betting on horses.

We wouldn't drink gin and tonics frantically,
the way our ancestors brought in crops
when they knew it was going to frost.
We wouldn't drink anything but tea.

After one or two cups, I'd read the leaves
from the present (rim by the handle)
to our deep, Cimmerian futures in the dregs.
But we'd know what our futures held;
the children at our breasts would know too.
We wouldn't inhabit the land of perpetual darkness.
We'd believe in the joys of Heaven; have no other choice.

I turn my attention to the band of greasy guys in the corner
as though I care desperately for aggressive thrash,
opening bars of *Enter Sandman*—try to figure out
which I'll bum a cigarette from at two or so
when it's time to tear down and say goodbye.

Water

Laid off from Union Tool,
he's Muddy Water's brand of *ready*.

No more pitchforks, open fire.
No more paycheck either,
but perhaps even this, a blessing.

Why shouldn't he start over at 50?
Cast his net to the other side?

Mohawk River's lovely this time of year.
Canoe downstream to Lock 18
and it's cedar waxwings, kingfishers—
a pair of bald eagles if you're lucky.

But he doesn't own a boat,
and the trail winds along the canal
where you can't see a damn thing.

Smoke from Route 5S finds its way
into the pocket of his flannel.
Crickets scatter. A lone crappie flops.

He could crack a can of Utica Club
on Casey, where there's always
a fire and a girl who knows

or move wife and sons
to Kentucky—pay is slim,
but cigarettes aren't taxed

like his back and maybe men
don't stoop like they've spent
their lives portaging barges.

Or if he cared about such things,
he could be baptized again.

He knows a few who've done it;
seen Jesus in a barmaid at Reggie's,
hills over the Valley.

As if aspersion, immersion,
even salvation itself could make up
for the shame of sitting in a class
full of college kids who don't know
this town is more than an exit
off the Thruway, trove

where you can mine for diamonds
that aren't really diamonds at all.

His ancestors settled this land;
survived massacres, revolution.
They figured things out.

How come all these years later
he's the indentured servant?

He'll drive up Vickerman,
try to make out his father's cross
through rain that falls like holy water
on vugs of quartz and granite.

Hawks

Winter's so simple; without leaves
you can see through oak groves
where red-tailed hawks hunt in tandem,
even off the New York State Thruway.

Now the blue squills are out,
raised beds wet from freshet;
wrens scramble for nest
and I'm not sure of anything.

I browse for used cars with low mileage
as though my life depends on a deal,
schedule real estate showings—
view farmhouses with gambrel barns,
grain silos when we don't know
how to grow anything but gray hair
and mold in our closets, cultivate
children who read too much,
dream not of soaring but falling.

Where is the exhilaration of spring?
The flush that drives our deepest
needs to the surface?
Why does everything hurt?
I can think of nothing
but those hawks, even when I know
damn well they're not lovers,
perched side by side, gazing hard
with red eyes at opposite fields.

The Musicians

She steals a walk
with the kids.
The park sparkles with glass;
a condom rides the swing.

He drags his guitar to the attic.
Landlord curses the smoke,
but shrinks to kick him
out; new amp's soaked
and the screaming
is becoming noiseless.

Soon, the box of wood
itself will wax inaudible,
long, untamed hair
will fell itself,
loud and pubescent,
into dangerous blessings
she'll bury under a tree for swallows.

Slava

Thanksgiving. Glory.

Emily was sleeping, so you drove me to Jordanville.
The woods were posted. You knew that,
but wanted one good look at the Rostropovich place.

It was fall. There was a lake, the kind you only find Upstate.
I held your hand, head on your shoulder, the firstborn.
You still had most of your hair, dark brown and curly;
you combed out the sides to make it seem more.

In twenty-five years, what has changed?
Same steel-toed boots, eye for seasonal beauty,
moustache you've always worn, save for the time
you shaved and I cried. I didn't know you.

You like to remind me that I've resisted change since the day I was born.

But since the day I was born again, all I want is change.
I dream in cello concertos, imagine art without borders
and freedom of speech, hope that someday, you too
will embrace a life only glimpsed from forbidden forests.

Then the castle on the hill will be inside
like a gift or perfect memory
and maybe you'll forgive your own trespasses
the way you've forgiven mine.

The Hills

Bees

For Chad and Jamie

For his coronation, Napoleon rejected
fleur-de-lis, token of French sovereigns.
To symbolize the power and prestige of his empire,
a jewel of greater antiquity: Bees.

The Sun King may have scorned the treasures
of Childeric, Merovingian monarch cadaverous
in 482, tomb forgotten until excavation 1200 years later—
its gold fibula, bull's head, cloisonné, crystal ball,

but the slight Corsican, known to laugh inappropriately,
pinch cheeks in salons rather than make small talk
would take the remains of a horse harness
studded with 300 gold *fleurons* as his emblem.

Bees in his coat of arms, embroidered onto his robes,
curtains, even his wife's satin slippers.
Bees of immortality, resurrection, linking
au courant with ancient history.

My experience with bees hasn't been so empyrean.
Still, in 1985, a downed weeping willow on my friend's
dairy farm became a fort worthy of a Bessie Smith song,
even, perhaps, of Corporal Violet himself.

We were a moth-eaten army, uniforms of half-shirts,
bicycle shorts, jellies caked in mud, cow manure.
We followed our barefoot leader from trunk to crown,
would have burned the garrison ourselves
had invaders ventured to take our city.

By the end of summer we were forced to retreat.
The hive had swelled; bees didn't care for our trade
agreements. My mother pulled a dozen stingers from
my head; my friend took an even harsher beating.

But after Drumsticks, he stopped crying,
ran out back to play with his sister;
everyone wished I'd follow suit. Bees.

    It's been four winters since his passing.
Still, a cold one on rations and rags is sometimes enough
to create cataclysm—banish insecure bullies to an island
in the Mediterranean, make room
for these recollections, however raw.
Like crystallized honey, may they be preserved for a century.

Dresses

Four vintage shifts, polyester prints,
matching sashes to cinch, loose
or tight through hyper-navel loops.

I wash them by hand,
soap and rinse and wring
until the skin lifts from my fingers,
swirls like slip lace into a pair of
barely there stockings which cover,
however flimsily, blue veins
like drainpipes, like boxes
that line old cellars.

She allows her tape to be cut,
a story for every skirt—
smock from London, Indian sarong,
1956, 1979. "*My* hippy days
were never confined to the sixties."

I suppose that mine,
if you can call them that,
were limited to college years,
that brief period of halter-top sewing,
mid-drift baring, patchouli wearing,
sage burning, burrito buying
and can't believe that was ever me—

barefoot in Buffalo for the Christmas show,
smoking world peace in the Swan St. garage
with some white kid with dreds,
desperate to predict Phish's setlist,
wondering if this time there'd be horns.

I think of who I am now: wife, mother,
gills greased on organic teas,
conservative champion of cloth diapers,
breastfeeding, the gauze kurta.
Last time I smoked anything I fell into sleep,
dreamed a great horned owl took off in a storm.
I know both signs; they mean death.

It's the cotton that resists change,
does not want to be clean.
Must clings to cloth-covered buttons
and bell-sleeves, gathered at the wrists.
Hope-colored shirtwaists bleed in cold water,
and I wonder if she'll be gone soon,
if she's remembered to retain anything
to be buried in, or if she'll sell them all
to Gen-Xers like me, some who will wear
and cherish, others who'll barter
and re-sell until history hangs on wire,
upscale thrift shop in Park Slope.

Her soul ascends, though she still has form.
Like the starched collar of a mother hubbard,
this heavenly journey seems pointless—
if the dress had no shape to begin with,
why force an afterlife.

When I go, let me be naked
save a mood ring and dark lipstick.
I may no longer care if the band
stays together, or even where I go
when my seams have been sewed
for the very last time, but will always
believe in that early nineties shade.

In the end, a promise is made:
to let the dresses lead,
to listen to their legacies.
But the ones I've bought
are for work and church,
where I cannot perform the jerk bra-less.

Cathy

Letters sting like white spiders
in boxes, in closets,

with red seals like blood,
with blood that is yours;

In my pretty handwriting
I'm spilling a song

with some ships and cradles,
an evergreen tree

on my next resume
so they know I'm a cast off,

a fondly yours—
living in prisms and moors.

Trestle

(Newly Engaged, 1997)

We peal and snort through Highland Park,
send a few ground hogs under the lilacs,

gray squirrel into mountain laurel,
heron to perch on Frederick Douglass

whose face, through blue feathers,
lets me know that this laughter's inculpable,

clean, corrective—
this dreaming that's above good sense

like a natural arboretum, in whose sunken garden
freedom fighters wear their hair long,

or a fishplate cross-tying two sleepers,
railroad conceived of a star.

Fluff

You'd think I ripened
under a poplar

the way fluff gets stuck
in the crevices,

clogs synapses,
makes a memory shift

and grow like the pistil
of a purple-flowering raspberry

into a hundred drupelets
until I can no longer recall

what truly happened
that night in the snow;

do you know?
Do your lips still linger

in the flowstone
of Steele Creek

as travertine
counts the time

in amber rings,
translucent cross-sections?

Envy

Your wife's a bumblebee
    in the best sense, constant.

She laughs like a home
    and gardens columnist,

one concerned with gadgets,
    the mundane: miniature

windmills spinning
    for moles half blind.

Humanely, they'll eliminate
    backyard pests

and past loves,
    through vibration

send hangers-on running.
    And you can't blame a man

for craving rhubarb pie
    over poems that burrow

deeper into earth each winter,
    sometimes motionless

though never dormant
    gnawing worms, drying out

roots and hoping
    beyond reason

they're still binary, complex
    as this drunken dog star,

buzzing constellation
    you once called beautiful.

Sarabache

It was always dangerous—dry grass and briers,
deer scat and ice. But there was something
about that hill covered in snow; and to those
of us with scanty town yards, meager as our
fathers' factory paychecks, it was Lucky 7:

at night, a country song, constellation,
by day, a quartz crystal, Herkimer diamond.
It stuck out its chest and wasn't ashamed;
that flat belly went on for what seemed miles.

Now it's cinderblocks, tar and tires—
a bus route behind the elementary school,
Francesca's *St. Agatha*, because parents are afraid
to let children walk, because of Sara Ann Wood,
because the younger generation isn't going to mass.

When they carved Sarabache, I was away at college,
head packed like a pipe with melting clocks
but someone else was getting high,
and sallow smoke pouring from my mouth
tasted like something I once knew and loved.

Swan Bones

> "Occupy till I come."—LUKE 19:13

Somewhere in the center
of star formation,
freezing in fingerless gloves,
we blew hot air
into silver flutes,
tiny apertures—
breathed and stared
at field markers,
yellow and cold,
wet like the ground
a moment from frost.

How quickly fall nights
become potsherds,
and memories,
even the most bromidic,
excavation sites.

Thirty thousand years
the swan bone sat,
the mammoth tusk,
femur of a bear—
ancient instruments biding time:

cavities ready to resonate,
holes to be blown over,
occupying until,
not a moment too soon,
a savior comes.

In late October,
sick of the wait,
a color guard
ditches sparkle velvet
swing flags on the fifty
as if to proffer resignation
from this universal parade
of work and rest,
blind to the beauty of satellites,
predictability in the night sky,
pulchritude of planets.

And being fifteen
and having no compassion
for puffins and plumes,
I consider the northern gannets
off the Ayrshire coast,
those capacious,
powerful white birds
with the light blue bills,
black wings—
find comfort in
their clumsy take-offs,
gawkish landings,
taste for crags and granite.
Hope that I,
like the diehard booby,
will stick with something
or someone
for at least a few seasons.

Song for Red Efts

"Everything belongs." —Fr. Richard Rohr

We ripped them from Davis Mountain,
delicate as lady slippers, adolescent salamanders
we'd coarsen on crickets, night crawlers, the faith of a child.

How did we think they could live?

But we rode our bikes and made love, formed
a terrarium for our treasures to approximate wild, original earth.

By late October, two were dead, long nights spent
upending cement blocks in search of food. I prayed for a worm—
for the smallest, lowliest sign this was not the end.

In our Eastern-most forests there's crawl space for spots,
for half-grown spirits but it was cold that November,
sun and no clouds. No one to tell us that everything belongs.

Releasing the remnant, five or so into the Churchville Reservoir
we wept the way you must when you've covered
your dreams in fig leaves, body in symbols and stories.

Hats Off

> "The Middle Falls, called 'Ska-ga-dee,' was so beautiful that
> it could stop the sun at midday, so the Seneca thought."
> —Catskill Clear

The antique place is no different from any other in the county:
Popeye salt and pepper shakers, *Shit Creek Survivor* shot glasses,

Ferrante and Teicher records penned in by misogynistic sports
dross: decoy pintail ducks, Cabela's hunting catalogues.

But this kid loves hats. Balmorals, berets, *capuchons*.
Has an eye for French ribbonwork; metallic net and silk roses.

Oh budding milliner, this is a small town
where women pull baseball caps over cockled eyes,

even virgin rims reek of Marlboro smoke
and most folks would rather dally at the Dollar General

than drive ten miles down the Genesee to Portage Canyon,
falls so majestic the Seneca believed they could make the sun stop.

Cloches, fedoras, trilbies, chimney pots, porkpies, beanies.
Why are you still here? Everyone knows what common

moths do to cashmere, still you're pinning on feathers,
dreaming of hats as you turn weathered face to the sun.

Black Caps

For Alden S. Gallogly

Black caps surround the cemetery.
For years, I considered this strange.
Who would eat fruit
made perfect by death?

And yet my mother walks the canal path
every summer with a basket
in search of these wild raspberries
which will stain her fingers and culottes,
and whose thorns will rip at her wrists like a barn cat.

She says that monarchs,
in their migration to Mexico,
can take all they need to fly
from the waste of geese,
that in Madagascar,
there's a moth which feeds
off of the tears of birds,
that there's even a name for it—
mud-puddling.

I understand what my mother means.
When we lose someone we love,
we must figure out a way
to turn memories into nutrients
for our souls, substrates into wings.

I think of what you left behind:
endless numbers of junk cars
in the back field, a camper,
a school bus
you meant to fix up

but never did,
three coffee pots
when Grandma drinks tea,
Reader's Digest jokes,
recited so many times
at the funeral, I think
I'll never laugh again.

How I want to jump onto
your '48 Indian,
ride until I reach
the homestead, the canal,
the Fort Herkimer church, the black caps.

But the motorcycle's long gone,
and the house, razed;
we figured you were too brittle
to keep mowing around granite
and lilacs, the passing of time.

Still my best friend knows
this is where I need to be.
She drives, brings wine.
(It's too early for berries,
even a burial,
and you will not return
to the ground until spring.)
She opens the bottle in the gazebo
that stands just yards
from the ghosts and pillars
of my childhood.

I think of the gifts you gave,
the elements:
Sunday roasts with salt potatoes,
ice cream sandwiches like stars,
or descendants—too numerous to count.
"Can I get you anything?" you'd say,
even in the hospital, dying.

I wonder if I'll ever be able
to take these gifts, what you left, and fly.

We drink under the planets,
Venus, Jupiter,
with fear and trembling.
We stare into the Barge Canal,
our breath like brush-footed butterflies,
at black cap bushes,
the old belfry, the old sky.

Casey Road

For years I saw you through the smoke of an open fire,
but only now are you becoming crepuscular,
a moonflower or bat, opening petals, spreading wings
and devouring nearly invisible pests that would eat me
alive now I know something of the world outside the Valley.

Your camber is legendary. You arch and curve
and in doing so, lessen effects of centrifugal forces,
constant threat of layoffs, lack of scope.
The week runs off your back like rain.

From the beginning of time, before continents shifted
from friendly neighbors to lonely santons
you were begging outside newsrooms,
whirling for a child with tobacco-stained fingers

who'd rather die than surrender this ghost
of a crossroads, vestige of vespertine:
In your barrels he'll burn, by echolocation,
find a girl with big tits in total darkness.

Like Dinah, I left this town, my father's,
only home I've ever known. I raged against it.
Was too smart for it. And what has been accomplished?

A king's son steals what was already lost,
last leaves fall on the New York State Thruway,
and Casey is under two feet of snow.
Utica Club on their lips, my brothers will have their revenge.

Dineen's

(After Fishing)

Like a trolling spoon
she'll lure him—

wobble,
    flash,
        catch light

under the vintage Genesee beer sign;
Aphrodite with a pool cue.

Dollar Tree eyeliner's
silver as scales.

He'd like to remove it,
but only knows

how to clean
asbestos from popcorn ceilings.

Why has no one taught these two to dance?

Imitate the movements
of a crippled minnow.

Pick second chances
from a generous beard.

Burn,
    sparkle,
        scream.

In the dream, a simple game
of darts chips away

at a heart cavity so friable,
dust particles collect in my gills,

lungs like a sad song on the juke box,
one you can't stop humming.

Red '86 Honda Nighthawk

For Daniel

That kid, whatever his name was, crashed it the week you sold it,
singeing the clout from your calves for at least a cold season.
It was money for college, the bus, coffee and cigarettes.
It was red, a 650, big. Rode the way Pete Maravich shot,
averaging 44.2 per game in drooping socks.
More sac than you needed, with that tousled hair
and chip on your shoulder wishing *your* dad had shone
a flashlight just once, guarded you from that most pressing
need to practice control tricks, head fakes on wheels
but he didn't have a father. Didn't know how to be one.
And you were difficult as dazzling. You knew it even then;
had to get out before you cracked because one day
you'd be ready to free legend, forgive shadows fastening
you pointlessly to the foul line, Union Tool pitchforks,
the open fire, whatever his name was and is and just
maybe remember the past as a series of beautiful rides.
You'll launch poems now; run with your burdens.
It's no longer raining and the Ilion Gorge is waiting
as it has been for three cursed generations and the light
shines on the waters of the West Canada and you're free!
Free to buy another bike better suited to your physique,
to quit drinking. Free to get out, not just in body
but in the spirit of one who was raised from dead.
Free to not die before you are forty. Accept the good
with the ugly. Slow down. Listen triumphantly
to the Louis Armstrong record collection inherited
from your grandfather who loved that man's voice
as much as he hated leaving you, his wife, this hard Valley.

Woman with Outstretched Arms

Picasso Sculpture at MoMA, 2016

So different from the woman in *Guernica*,
born not of bombs and warplanes
but paper maquettes, those old animal
figures you used to cut for your sisters.

Her face, an owl's; pubic hair your first
mistress's: *La Belle Fernande*—
girl you rescued and woman you locked up.
She knew you blue, before crystals and cubes,

before the twinkles in your eye became
cocks in the ring for a legacy. Did you
think of her later? More than anything
she wanted a child. And she got one,

sure—paltry thing from the home
returned the minute she knew you
were painting her too, realized
there would always be a younger,

more beautiful muse, dreams still intact.
My dreams are intact. Breasts, full.
But not as they could be, were they fashioned
of scrap metal, bolstered with talons and feathers.

Potpourri

Lamb's ear, rose-hip, orange peel, cinnamon.
Orris root to preserve, essential oil just in case;
we want these dead flowers to last.

Why not extend the life of the rotten pot?
Make it sing with archangels forever and ever?

Give me a fixative when I die
so my essence releases slowly.
Let me dry well, morph into the farrago.

Maybe then, I'll become more palatable—
preferably with wings, a good voice.

But if not, if someone forgets to add
spices and mold sets in with its filaments:
a breakdown colorful as sunrise.

Casting on Loon Lake

He shoots snapshots at dusk
with wide angle lens and flashlight,
loads line onto spinning reels
as blue heat burns wet wood,
cracks and sparks and cracks.

She smokes American Spirits,
travis-picks his guitar
as Northern bats fly low over the lake
and loons try to remember
the lyrics to last year's love song.

Please give her slack.
Get her best side, silver in her braid.
But before the shutter's triggered,
let there be a delay:

Those fifteen minutes supplanting
sundown are magic and won't linger
for the baleful whir of black flies.

So if by chance you remember the words
to the one song you ever gamboled to,
climb into the row boat, release the line
and troll them out in buccinal baritone.

Country Affair

For A.

I want to be top couple
at the country dance,
know pure refreshment,
shoot in the morning.

Instead, I sit like a widow
in crape and bombazine,
surveying my husband's
cornfields, razed by hounds,
lambs sacrificed for sport.

You sit astride a hunter,
drink claret.
Wipe fox blood into my cheeks
like it's the first time.

Is it so hard to see me,
your linnet, your bird?
I too can be red in summer.

If I were a man I'd run,
not for brushes or masks,
nothing dead or holding
its breath in a covert
of thicket and gorse—

wouldn't be so quick
to jump a white fence
beyond which I can't even dream.

But I'm here, leading this set,
whether I want to or not,
away from the door—
guiding old and new friends
around dripping wet horses.

Blueberries

Nine-Cornered Lake,
you've come back to us:
Hope in the form of midge larva,
minute as an eyelash on my cheek
and yet even the blueberries
which grow wild this season
seem to know a wish has come true.

For decades you were dead.
I shed bell-shaped tears
waiting for pale green to turn red,
purple to indigo, dreamed
of that fruit with the flared crown
(but never really hoped for more than
a borrowed tomb sealed with lilies.)

Slowly, that stone's been rolled away.
Scrubbers, Clean Air,
and it's the miracle
of berries and brook trout.
Here come the pH, the bears.
This resurrection's electric;
dry bones dance in Fulton County.

But we're not out of the woods yet.
Unsinkable premonition
change won't tarry long before
hightailing it back to Albany,
city without black flies.

Coal still burns at 1000 degrees.
Alternating currents produce acid rain
and sometimes, even armies of pine
are no match for the Heartland.

Black bears survived the last Ice Age
with sharp senses, long memories—
somehow followed their mothers
to Nine-Cornered Lake,
base of the Adirondacks.
They came back.

They returned with sweet tooth
like my son, our first communications
in the sign language of blueberries:
Do you like them?
Grins. Shaking of legs.

I too have eaten yellow jackets,
endured the Upstate winter,
shoveled with blistered hands

but always hoped this was not the end—
that July would come, and with it
a restocking so filled with sun
anything could rise again.

Here come the loons;
the fish have stayed.
Here come the kids,
wet towels and cigarettes.
I want to believe this will last.

We wake up,
reach for a warm beer,
site a mess of empties.
Forget who drummed naked
in the circle, remember
the cadence for all of time.
We buffer, pollute.
Evolve in water.

The omnivore approaches;
his eyesight is keen.
We'll see who gets there first.

Advent Ride

Some nights in early December
nature is Scripture—a barred owl
shaking snow from its wings,
some of which melts in my braid.

It's snowmobiling down a trail
whose name Anne might have hatched
on the buggy ride from orphanage to home,
bosom friends, amethyst brooches, books.

It's stopping by a red oak for a burl
fat as a wasp's paper nest;
not to tap it, no matter how biblical
it would look as clock or bowl,
nor slice into veneer what defies sculpting.

Boiled for days, its sap would remain
like its grain, twisted, wild.

Is it only here, in these gelid, boreal woods
one can know what Anne must have guessed then?

That The Word always springs from sacrifice,
burl from malignancy, and pregnancy—
even the immaculate kind—from pain?

The Valley

Butterfly

> "And it came to pass in those days, that Jesus came from Nazareth of Galilee, and was baptized of John in Jordan. And straightway coming up out of the water, he saw the heavens opened, and the Spirit like a dove descending upon him."—MARK 1:9-10

Straightway coming up out of the water
of Peter-Bob's above ground pool,
snot dripped down my early-eighties
color-blocked swimsuit, chlorine
from my braids and I saw her—
Heather—one year older, complete
with coveted Dorothy Hamill wedge.
Always winning tops for memorizing
scripture. Mary in the Christmas pageant.

I thought that after I went under,
sins washed away, I'd cease imagining
Heather as a galley slave from Ben Hur,
heroin addict from my strangely approved
comic, *The Cross and the Switchblade*.

And me, I'd be transformed—
Much Afraid to *Grace and Glory*.
No longer too shy to witness
to my fellow first-graders
and maybe, just maybe, clothed
in righteousness so bright
my hand-me-downs and glasses
would be cast, like sins, into the sea.

When I emerged from the pool
the sounds were geotic; guitars
and tambourines and I knew what
I had to do: swim.

Heather couldn't swim.
I would show them all:
crawl, breast stroke, butterfly.
Anointed with the Holy Ghost
I'd swim. Renewed in Christ
I'd swim. "He gave me new life,
something to hope for,"
my mother's pellucid alto.
Something to hope for.
I hung my head as pastor lifted
my skinny shivering body from blue water.

Candles, Sugar, Rum

The church we were married in
is historic, a bulwark on the Mohawk.
It's also a double-edged sword,
boasting transparency and whiteness,
seeming infallible when if fact,
it has made a killing for generations
off the selling of fortunes:
Foreign language tips in back
(Sex! Unity! Mystery!)
and lucky numbers in front,
Revolutionary stones—
gray slate skipped across the canal
by a child-like god.

Two-hundred years past fighting time
he's hiding in clefts and mortar
a misspelled truth,
sucking on whole crops of sugarcane,
shooting spit-wads at our tassels and cannons.

Separate stairways descend from the pulpit;
years ago I thought this cold.
More beautiful secrets hid
in ladies' ankles and you,
bleeding General Herkimer
over our uniforms, still pointing the way
up Vickerman Hill where your grandmother
waits for light, a snake on a rock,
coiled in dirt and gold.

Marble City Breakdown

My faith is not a winner. It smokes in root cellars,
earns community cash at a "this-n-that" sale,
cash that demands attention—prestige of talc-miners
mumbling out the corners of their mouths,
short words, to the point,
saving black lung for their families
in case the army base pulls out.
It tacks plastic over rose windows
in winter, sprinkles rock salt
on the steps of St. James'.
It's a mustard-seed sub at Anamelia's;
needs one new business to last.
Still it's clapping in our pews—
getting its hair cut, ragged nails cleaned
in case the Promised Land is kicking
in a pregnant girl, in case someone important sees.

Wrestler

Winningest coach gets sacked
for a few hundred cups of spit,

striated, cavernous chests
on boys who should, statistically,

be long-haired and dimpled,
tobacco stains on fingernails

grown long enough to pick a guitar,
pump out those three-chord

blessings of our times, the ones
that make us strain and grunt

and strive while the wrestler,
the jock, spends his nights creating

kinesthetic harmonies, strumming,
muting, plucking out six-minute

symphonies we know nothing of
in our culture of dribbles

and dunks where there's always
a teammate to pass the ball to,

teacher to blame when we
lock hands, flee the mat.

Blue Lens

Mexico City, 2004

She shapes balloon animals,
paints cheeks while her husband
runs refraction tests with a
phoropter from the seventies.

All the kids want *espadas*,
swords resembling gigantic
penises or blue crosses;
half a day before she realizes
it's a football club
not a sign of Christ.

What propels her through
975 acres of landfill
is also blue—*Casa del los
Azulejos*, 18th century
House of Tiles.

Eight hours later
she'll eat *mole*
in a clean, pressed skirt,
stroll past street vendors
and a spray paint artist
creating eight-minute
masterpieces on Masonite.

With fire, he'll dry
the planets: cold dust
particles hang
in the Hadeon Eon,
bombarded by meteorites,
dreams of a half-dozen
elderly fitted with cat eyes.

Baptism

By mid-February I've tossed Sunday
to a homeless man.
My garment of praise is
a memory of one hot night.
Despite all this,
considering our daughter's baptism,
tardy dove offering,
I'm comforted.

By mid-August, Patna is
ready to be pushed under water,
ready for change.
Paper lamps paint doorways
on Coconut Day, outside the laundry
where women sing hymns like
they know they are clean:

Praise to the Creator.
Praise to the Destroyer.

Sound carries so well
in these valleys I wonder:
Who's the one with the blue throat?
Who's the one swallowing sin?
In my heart, the only law
is snow in Western New York.

The Bell

We hang you at equinox, fifty degrees and fair—
check the window every ten minutes to make sure
you're still there, ringing on that wick forsythia
a tone that can only be recognized by one who's known
oil and millet, one still trying to find her song.
Satisfied you'll hold fast, we stroll to the playground,
remember metal, rope, the dizziness of swings.

It snows the next morning. Your heart may be fashioned
of sunflowers, but mine's frangible, flagging—
hands callused, shoulders tight as a gray woman's jeans;
how she grasped geodesics yesterday, flipped and
climbed, shirt un-tucked, belly striped as a wild animal.

Seeds scatter to the ground; chickadees find them, wrens.
Still, the hope for a redpoll, flicker this bell's known to attract.
Forty is not so old.

Not a week and you're gone; not even a shroud remains.
Gray squirrel who filched my apple core earlier this month
has likely absconded with you. Sorry birds.
The kids are off from school, build a snowman
instead of mourning your loss as I'm bound to,
despite this lesson I'm still learning:

It doesn't matter whom the seed bell was meant for
when someone ate it, and for a moment was satisfied.

Wood Sorrel

She rips two handfuls, roots and all,
from loam holding tight our foundation.
She slips three times trying to climb onto
the hood of our friend's tired sedan,
still holding onto three-leafed clover
like she knows the religious significance
of each heart: hope, faith, love.
As she eats them one by one,
no one can look away; she is lucky enough,
blessed by this holy trinity.
She chews and swallows sweetness
some have spent their lives believing
can't be chymified—she offers it
up to them roots and all.
When they shake their heads,
pat threadbare pockets for matches,
she secures the common trefoil
under a wiper blade and someone lights
a rejected dove, the only fruit of his labor.

Luthier

An extra bridge, peculiarly placed pickup,
fretless plexiglass guitar—
he conceives only specialty models,
begets only first born sons.

From the courts of King Saul
to Ulster Hall, Belfast, 1971—
where Jimmy Page let the whole world
know twelve strings on top can slay
any giant—his stairways.

And what are they worth now?
Markets have changed, and nobody cares
about the getting there, clamber, or jam;
double-necks are heavy,
and just when do you play one anyhow?

Still, a slingshot full of pebbles,
smooth arms for lanate
and every hope and dream has shifted.
Grasping at heels, the supplanter:
Posturing in front of the mirror,
a star with his Squier Fat Stratocaster.
He knows nothing of Old Testament anti-heroes,
singular gods who create *ex nihilo*,
but strums the G chord like a warrior king lover,
comes like a whammy bar in soft tremolo.

Angelica

The church is courthouse, armory,
gym, polling place, Grange.
On Monday nights, in the sanctuary,
Holly leads Zumba.
Weekends, it's crafts:
rosary pliers for crimping,
and cold metal sounds holy
as the hills over the Genesee,
inviolable as kids shooting snowballs
into the belfry. They wait
for the bus, one young mom
in pajamas jump starting another.

The church is more communal
than cigarettes, but there are bats
in the walls behind sheetrock,
their guano paints the baptismal
and Holly's had enough.
Time for a trailer with land,
life far removed from
antique-shop gossips, GEDs.

Asbestos crumbles under filigree,
glaciers erode into smoke,
and the truth about this town
lies under three layers of wallpaper.
At least here there's history.
People still pray for jobs
on the work crew. People still pray.
Once a year: Lions Club Turkey Raffle,
Lavender Fest, *Luminaries* Living Nativity.

All Souls

My neighbor beads rings and choke collars,
mows her mom's lawn and has, after years of exorcisms
made peace with the ghosts on the third floor of her Victorian.

Some nights, I hear them. She blows into her husband's
high school saxophone and they're laughing, dancing, knocking
over her craft table. The music drifts through my son's curtains

as I nurse him to sleep. Their story fills me with something like hope:
40-something artist meets 20-something environmentalist-
firefighter in village post office one must walk to in order to get mail.

They fall in love. Get married. Move into this big old place.
She continues with her jewelry. He rescues animals.
But it seems every time he goes, bats get in, and she hates bats.

Bats get in and so do the ghosts—small girl she believes tumbled
down the steep narrow steps and an old, skinny hunched man.
When she tells me about the ghosts, I can't sleep.

When I nurse my son, I close the curtains, bolt the window.
She didn't accept the ghosts overnight. She tried to get rid of them,
I tell myself. She's brave. She's crazy. I'm afraid. Of bats too.

They're usually babies, her husband says. They get in through the attic
at the end of summer, don't know any better. If you build a bat house,
they'll go there. If you open the windows, they'll fly out on their own.

But sometimes they're too young to know this. They dart around
all night only to perch someplace high and out of sight all day,
repeat this pattern over and over until one day you're doing laundry

and there it is, this helpless thing, your biggest fear, not quite dead.
Here's your chance to dig up welding gloves, place this little one
in your palm and walk it outside to the cedar hedge because you know

damn well they can't take flight from the ground. You pray
that somehow, in the end, this small grace will be enough to save
your soul, your son's soul, her soul, this small town's big haunted soul.

Betty

In every family,
one who remembers
birthdays—
gives laughable,
unimaginable gifts
ordered from QVC,
or with coupons off the back
of a Campbell's soup can.

In every family,
badly taken
photographs—
heads cut off,
souls reduced
to outmoded hair-styles.
Permanents rising
like ghosts,
out and up and all around.

Aunt Mary Stirs Coffee with Her Thumb

"cause nobody but a logger stirs his coffee with his thumb"
—"The Frozen Logger," James Stevens, Ivar Haglund

For every graduation, wedding, birthday:
a song. Silly lyrics paired with the tune of
The Merry Wanderer, William Tell Overture,
or some cryptic childhood novelty from
Methodist Camp Aldersgate:
Green Grow the Rushes, O, The Frozen Logger.

It was music you had to grow up with
in this family to truly understand.
Most of the cousins got at least a few bars.

In Nick's, some quip about a fly ball, while
Em's touted her Sarah Brightman-like knack
for nailing notes higher than C above the staff.
Aunt Betty's strain probably contained
her taste for rocky road ice-cream, dirty cards.

God, it was embarrassing singing those songs.
Everyone had to have a copy, stand up, perform—
men on the bum bum bums, women on descant.
What a group of weirdos we must have been.

And what I really don't understand is how
a single woman like her, shy as hell,
shut up in that room with Hershey's Kisses,
Camelot posters, Ray Bradbury novels
and a giant stuffed Simba insisted on it

year after year, with the tenacity of
The Logger: Venturing into a blizzard
at 100 degrees below zero,
he "buttoned up his vest."

After a dozen or so verses,
botched surgeries, stints in the ICU,
MRCA, my aunt finally succumbed too.
I guess it's ironic, the nor'easter
that kept me from her deathbed.

My mom put the phone up to her ear, though.
Said she stirred when my sister,
8-year-old daughter and I harmonized
from hundreds of miles away
to *I'll Fly Away, Castle on a Cloud*—
those hopeful melodies appropriate
for the end of things.

We skipped the goofballs she really loved:
*Sweet Nelly Bliss, Granny's in the Cellar,
The Frozen Logger*—

that guy falls so hard for a woman
he forgets everything else,
even his mackinaw, stupid virulent pride.

Communion

We are brown bears. We only leave each other alone
once a year, but on Christmas Eve, oh my.
There's fish enough for everyone, meat, bones
and we gorge ourselves, feast on miracles.

He made fish out of fish, loaves out of loaves.
In the cold, it's easy to forget this, forget
family, "salmon friends," even faith.

But we depend on this seasonal food
and wait for it on the other side of the boat,
game sanctuary of my grandparents'
country home around the piano.

For "The Carol of the Star," we each take parts.
The half-grown dive into the melody,
that melting ice, hope to blend in
so no one will hear their shaking voices,
notice their vulnerable necks.

The mothers hover around the descant.
They're not fat enough to sing low,
they've not spent the winter sleeping.

The fathers? They are the stars of the carol,
beloved disciples, favored pets.
Chip takes the solo; it jumps from his belly
like a silver chum salmon. He chews it
like a slippery scale; no one questions its beauty.

But even he is not above the law.
In the cold, he'll run after his young;
they will bleed from his mouth
like a song no one understands.

I don't understand. Still, I come to the table,
celebrate the birth of the son of God,
lean my head like John upon my father's shoulder.

Windows

She tries not to let the cold get her down:
stuffs pocket doors with Styrofoam noodle floats

(hopes they'll keep out starlings too),
drips faucets, cracks cupboards, seals the crawlspace.

Blankets block the stairs, but the second floor
has become warmer than the first, her head

an easier climate to dwell in. Here, the pipes don't burst,
basement doesn't flood and she's back in her hometown

mimicking the cry of every bird that's gone before her,
four-wheeling through fields of snow-dusted goldenrod.

But at night, the frantic song reprises and she wonders
if she's missed something. The windows: of course.

Bare, shrink-wrap free, they leak winter air and sun
with the same clear intensity. She will not give them up.

Shirley Jones and the Storm Cock

After an aphotic spell, a devotion arrives
from my mother's best friend, faithful
cultivator of Sisyphean flowers.
Intended to inspire, a psalm:
In the Lord I put my trust.

The rest sings the praises
of the mistle thrush, storm cock
common in the south of Ireland,
male of species known to perch
on the highest branch during a storm,
rattling and chattering like a ratchet,
loud, with short phrases rich and harsh.

I want to believe this, to trust
that this storm cock sings hurricanes
and earthquakes, even Charlottesville
because he loves the storm,
or if not, has hope through it—
unreasonable, overwhelming hope,
not because he's defending his territory,
is alarmed, disturbed, or even terrified.

I imagine his call quixotic,
nothing like a football rattle, machine gun;
more Claramae Turner belting
"You'll Never Walk Alone"
to a bereft Shirley Jones in *Carousel*.

I imagine it comforting: A kiss
on the corner of the mouth.
But even in musicals, carnival-barking
fathers strike their daughters
and I realize that I don't want blind hope—
ghosts or birds proffering promises.

Oh Louise Bigelow, don't take that star,
accept that song. Keep dancing, though.
Waltz on the beach, right through
the dream sequence, clambake, until light
finally breaks on this frail and fallen world.

Ram Offering

> "They pledged themselves to put away their wives, and their guilt offering was a ram of the flock for their guilt."—Ezra 10:19

> "...all the people sat in the open square...trembling because of the matter and the heavy rain."—Ezra 10:9

Over and over,
    the begats which really bless me.
Lists of names.

In the beginning,
    so many songs devoted to lineage.
Shooting stars.

These -ai ending names,
    soft on my lips as
bourekas almost

muffle those words in red:
    Anyone who loves his family
more than Me.

Oh Ezra, the blood is never enough.
    Not even in the days of prophets,
good kings and bad.

Repentance is turning your back
    on the child and its mother
every time—

putting away what is sundry,
 flowing, for the ease
of one true thing.

How is it that one prostrate man,
 tears in his eyes,
is worth more than a hundred,
 pumping?

Jiffy Lube Pam

"You related to Pam?" the mechanic asks
as I hand him my debit card, try not to smile
at his familiar accent noted the minute I sit
to wait for my high mileage oil change.
I try to recall what else my husband wants—
new air filter, I think, or is it a virgin vehicle,
garage that isn't a converted horse and buggy barn
so old its cement floor could easily crack after rain
from any one of our recent tornado watches.
That voice. Maybe not a North Country voice
but a workingman's voice: Closed mouthed. Direct.
So like my car-guy uncles', all back in New York
where they can't roll their eyes at us for not
changing our own oil, clemently do it themselves.
This guy has a sentimental streak too, reads
something other than space into my gap teeth,
thinks I'm one of the Indiana Bowmans
I've heard so much about since we moved.
I sign the receipt as he reminisces about
the HORDE tee Pam rocked back in '94;
strictly verboten from jam band-listening,
she mixed puff paint from flour, salt, water
and tempera to create an elephant monumental
as Dave riffing twenty minutes on *Watchtower*.
"I remember that show!" I find myself shouting.
No one knew the opening bars to the Dylan cover;
all these drunk idiots screamed for *Tripping Billies*
instead. "That's when things started to go downhill,"
he hands me a pen, and I know he's right and wonder if,
when *Crash* came out, he dubbed it for Pam and if so,
wasn't she a bitch for leaving this small town, her family,
guy with the voice still praying she'll breeze through these doors.

My Parents Jitterbug at Weddings

But most often slow dance on tired linoleum
those rare nights she bakes pies from rhubarb
the kids haven't already ravaged with sugar.

My parents jitterbug at weddings, but most often
swat mosquitoes on cool pavement, watch yellow
moonflowers open in the green space by the garage.

My parents jitterbug at weddings, but most often
Dad cuts across the cemetery to mow around
the gingko biloba that brings some cheer to my

grandmother's evening years. He'll try not to stew
about the jerk from his plant who won't let him
read on his lunch, try not to pick dead petals

off the dead's geraniums, as Mom sits in the glow
of the answering machine, plays back half a dozen
messages: requests for rides, prayer, piano.

My parents jitterbug at weddings, but most often
hold hands to say grace, which they insist
cannot be earned, as they toil, wait, and let go.

Mohawk Valley

Bees in the cupola,
moles in the garden,

sugar maples for
climbing and tapping,

ponds that aren't man made,
fish that aren't gold,

guitars and mandolins
bluegrassing, square dancing,

light strings that pop,
porches that tilt,

sinking foundations,
bobcat skeletons,

deer scat and muskrats,
Doc and Merle,

Woody and Huddy
with Emmylou Harris,

harmonies, lullabies,
long gray hair, big dark eyes,

clothespins that point to Polaris,
dippers to make the throat dry,

whisky to wash my prayers in,
Mohawk Valley when I die.